CLASSIC ROCK HITS

TAB EDITION

A No-Nonsense Approach to Playing 10 of Your Favorite Songs

How to Access the MP3 Play-Along Tracks on the Enhanced CD

Place the CD in your computer's CD-ROM drive.

Windows: Double-click on My Computer, then right-click on your CD drive icon and select Explore. Open the "Play-Along Tracks" folder to view the MP3 files. Double-click on a file to view it immediately or save it to a folder on your hard drive to view later.

Mac: Double-click on the CD volume named "TNT Song Player" on your desktop. Open the "Play-Along Tracks" folder to view the MP3 files. Double-click on a file to view it immediately or save it to a folder on your hard drive to view later.

About the TNT Feature on the Enhanced CD

You can use the TNT software on your enhanced CD to change keys, loop playback and mute the guitar for play-along. For complete instructions see the **TNT ReadMe.pdf** file on your enhanced CD.

Alfred Publishing Co., Inc.
16320 Roscoe Blvd., Suite 100
P.O. Box 10003
Van Nuys, CA 91410-0003
alfred.com

Copyright © MMIX by Alfred Publishing Co., Inc.
All rights reserved. Printed in USA.

For all works contained herein: Unauthorized copying, arranging, adapting, recording or public performance is an infringement of copyright. Infringers are liable under the law.

ISBN-10: 0-7390-5816-9 (Book & CD)
ISBN-13: 978-0-7390-5816-9 (Book & CD)

Cover Photos
Concert: © istockphoto/njmcc • Tie die: © istockphoto/Small Planet Photography

Recordings by the Chauncey Gardiner Combo, featuring Erick Lynen on vocals

Contents

Page	Title	Artist	Play-Along Track
	CD Tuning Track		1
3	Brown Sugar	The Rolling Stones	2
10	China Grove	The Doobie Brothers	3
15	Gimme Some Lovin'	Spencer Davis Group	4
26	Hotel California	Eagles	5
36	Layla	Derek and the Dominos	6
42	Lola	The Kinks	7
46	Maggie May	Rod Stewart	8
18	Moondance	Van Morrison	9
21	Sunshine of Your Love	Cream	10
50	Whole Lotta Love	Led Zeppelin	11
54	Guitar TAB Glossary		

BROWN SUGAR

*Elec. Gtrs. 1 & 2 tuned in Open G:
⑥ = D ③ = G
⑤ = G ② = B
④ = D ① = D

Words and Music by
MICK JAGGER and KEITH RICHARDS

Moderately ♩ = 126

Intro:

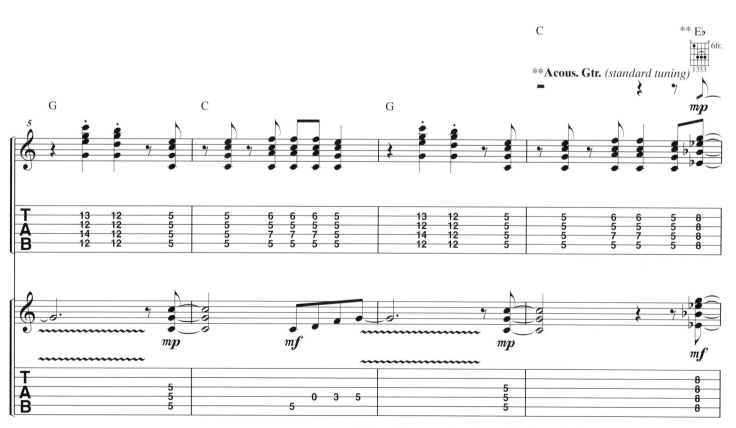

**Chord frames reflect Acous. Gtr. in standard tuning, entering at meas. 8.

© 1971 (Renewed) ABKCO MUSIC, INC.
All Rights Reserved

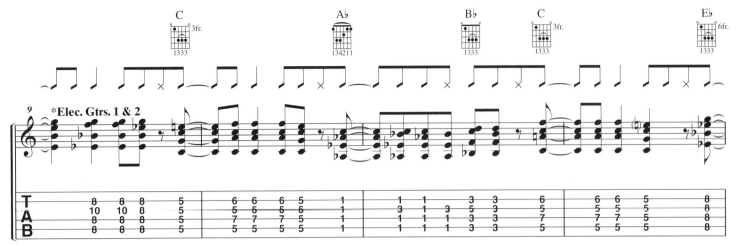
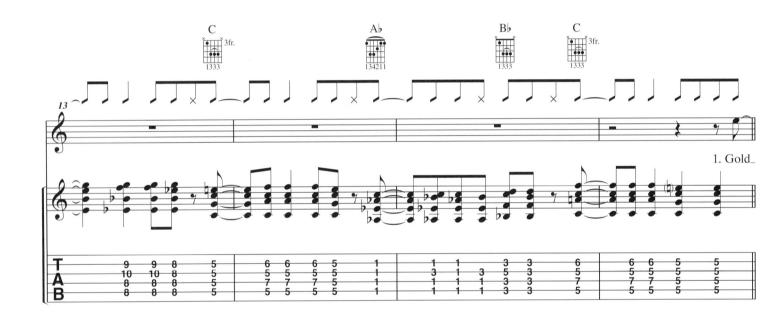
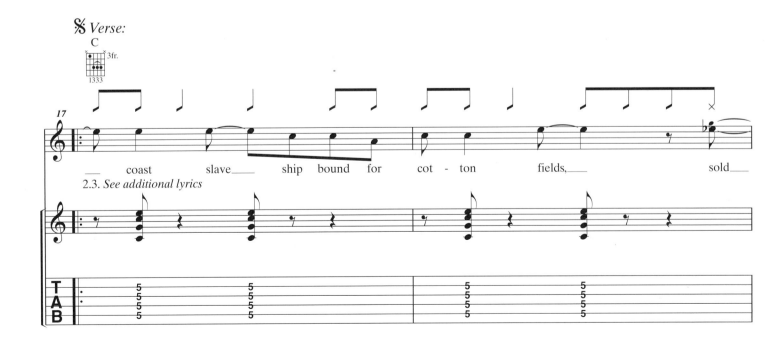

Verse 2:
Drums beating, cold English blood runs hot,
Lady of the house wondrin' where it's gonna stop.
House boy knows that he's doin' alright,
You should a heard him just around midnight.
(To Chorus:)

Verse 3:
I bet your mama was a tent show queen,
And all her boyfriends were sweet sixteen.
I'm no schoolboy but I know what I like,
You should have heard me just around midnight.
(To Chorus:)

GIMME SOME LOVIN'

Words and Music by
STEVE WINWOOD, MUFF WINWOOD
and SPENCER DAVIS

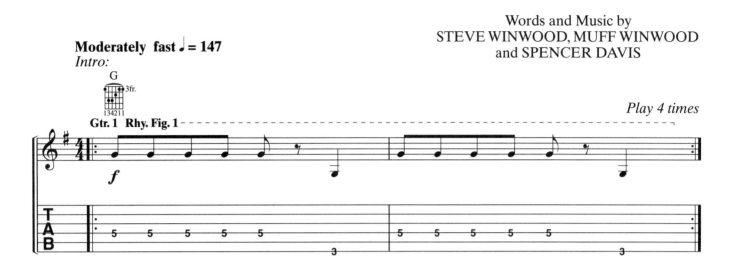

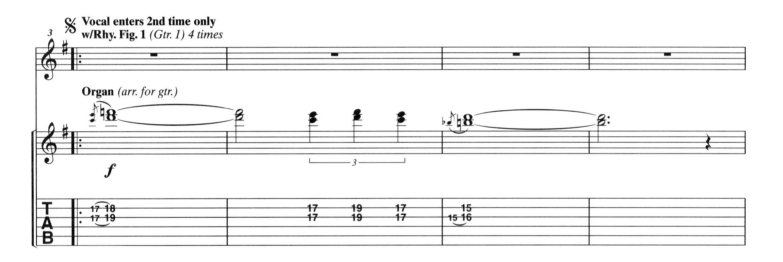

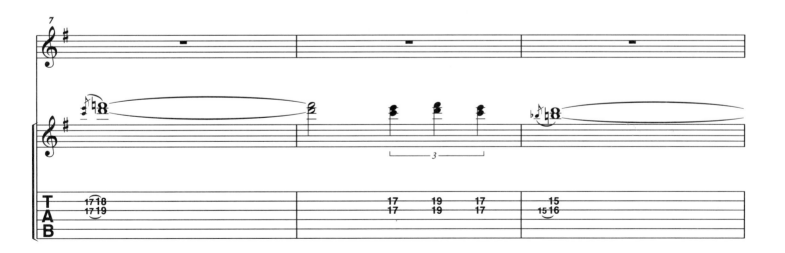

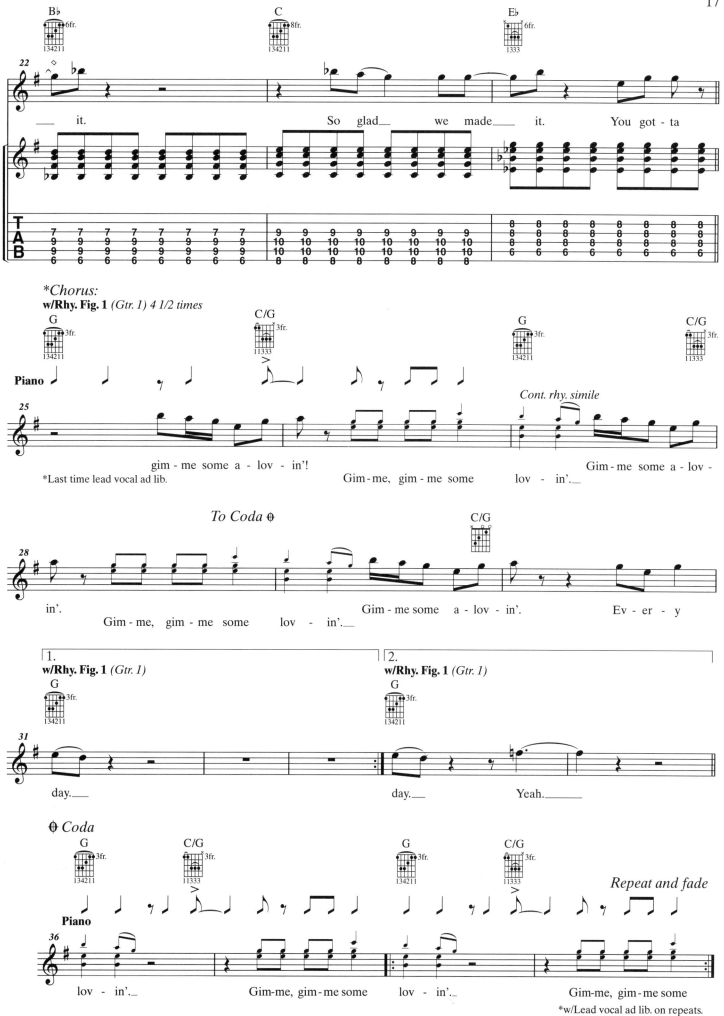

MOONDANCE

Words and Music by
VAN MORRISON

Moondance - 3 - 1

© 1970 (Renewed) WB MUSIC CORP. and CALEDONIA SOUL MUSIC
All Rights Administered by WB MUSIC CORP.
All Rights Reserved

SUNSHINE OF YOUR LOVE

Words and Music by
JACK BRUCE, PETE BROWN
and ERIC CLAPTON

Moderately ♩ = 114

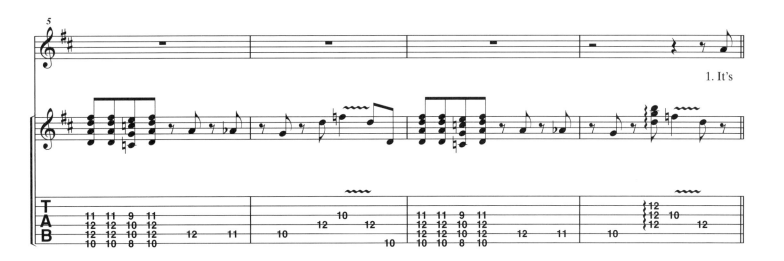

Sunshine of Your Love - 5 - 1

© 1968 (Renewed) WARNER/CHAPPELL MUSIC INTERNATIONAL LTD, DRATLEAF MUSIC, LTD. and E.C. MUSIC LTD.
All Rights in the U.S. for DRATLEAF MUSIC, LTD. and WARNER CHAPPELL MUSIC LTD. Administered by CHAPPELL & CO., INC.
All Rights Reserved

24

26

HOTEL CALIFORNIA

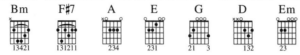

Chord frames reflecting concert key (for uncapoed gtr.)

Moderately slow ♩ = 74

Words and Music by
DON HENLEY, GLENN FREY
and DON FELDER

*Acous. Gtr. 1 w/capo VII, transposed to E minor.
Chord frames and TAB numbers relative to capo.
All other guitars w/o capo.
Chord frames w/italic names above represent capoed gtr.
Non-italic chord names under frames represent concert key.
Chord frames reflecting concert key appear under song title.

Hotel California - 10 - 1

© 1976 (Renewed) CASS COUNTY MUSIC, RED CLOUD MUSIC and FINGERS MUSIC
All Print Rights for CASS COUNTY MUSIC and RED CLOUD MUSIC Administered by WARNER-TAMERLANE PUBLISHING CORP.
All Rights for FINGERS MUSIC Administered by WB MUSIC CORP.
All Rights Reserved

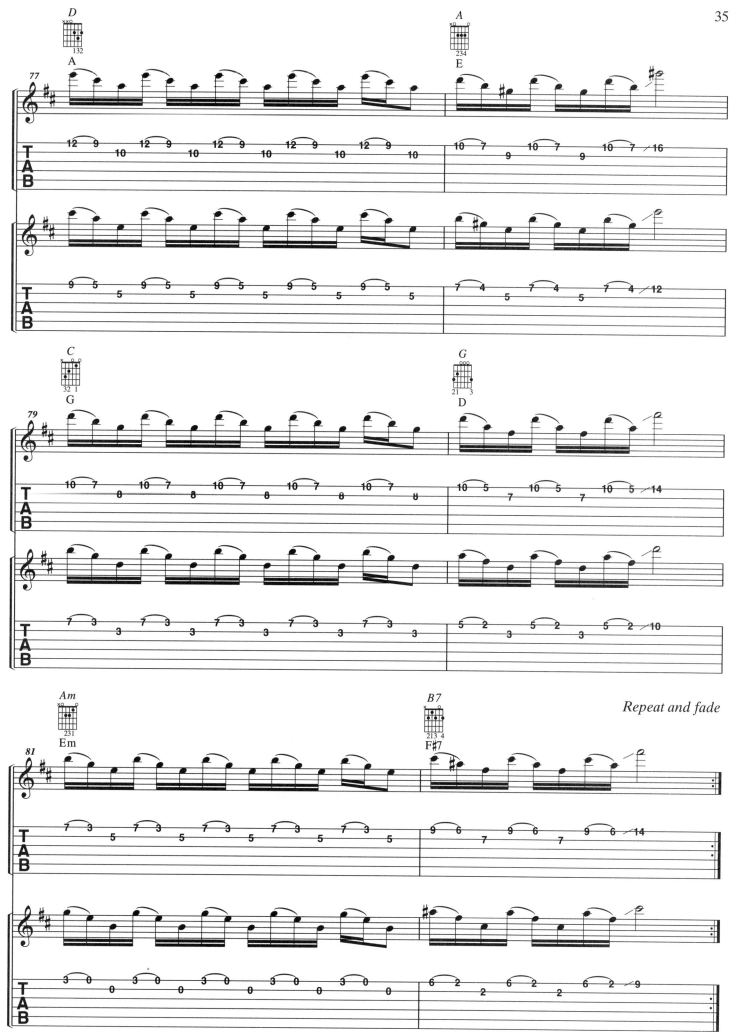

LAYLA

Words and Music by
ERIC CLAPTON and JIM GORDON

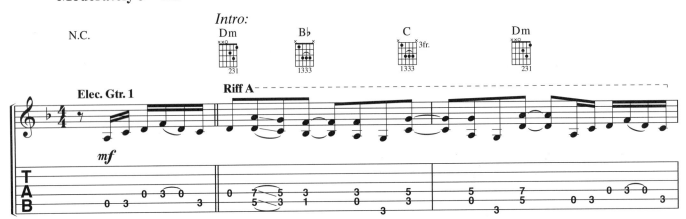

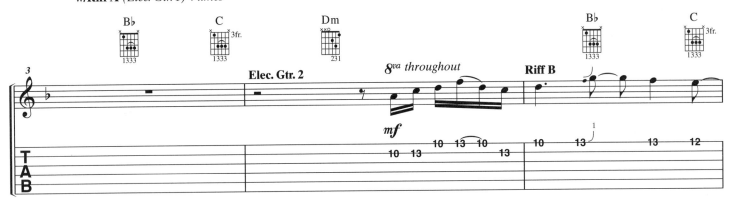

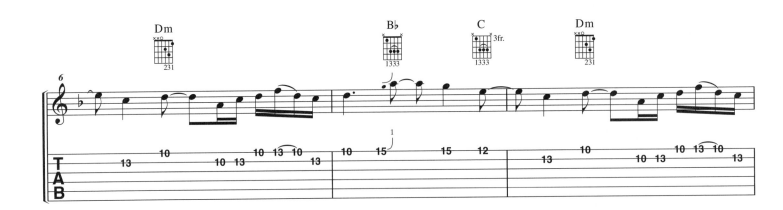

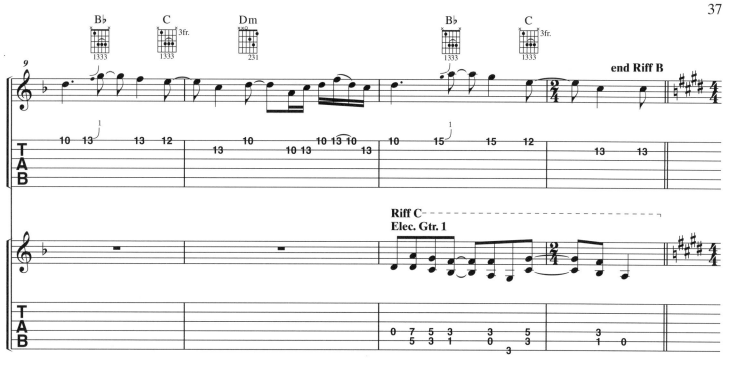

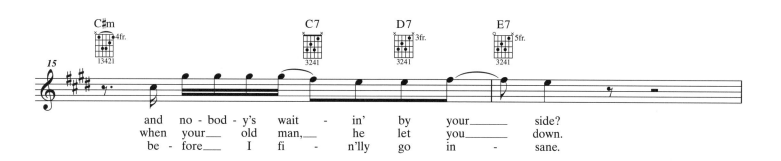

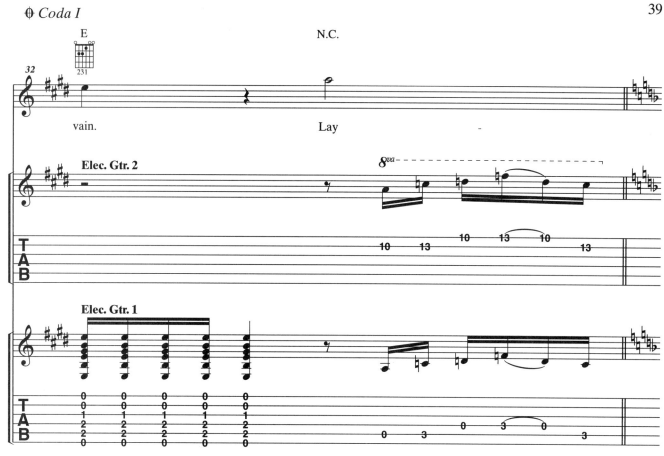

Chorus:

w/Riff A *(Elec. Gtr. 1) 4 times*
w/Riff B *(Elec. Gtr. 2) 1st 4 meas. only, 2 times*

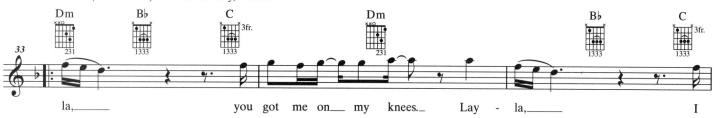

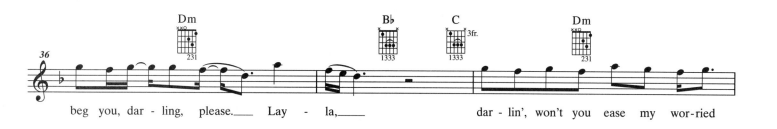

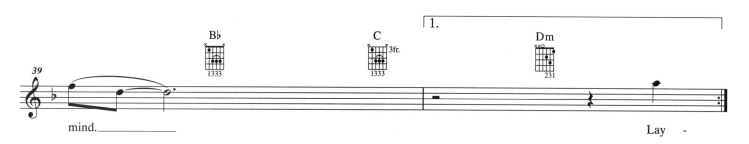

LOLA

Words and Music by
RAY DAVIES

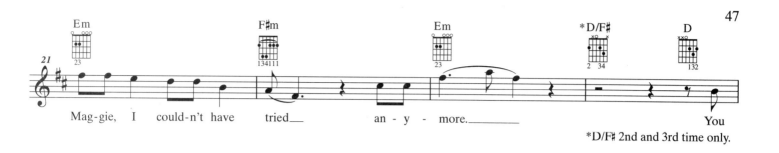

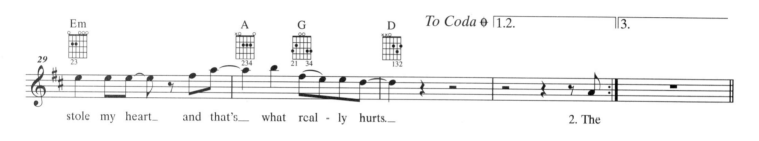
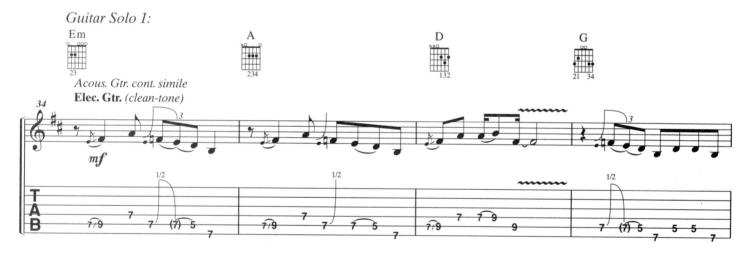
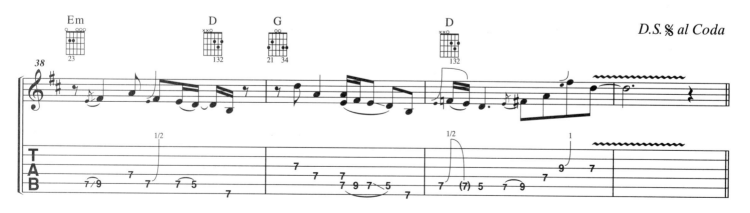

Coda

Guitar Solo 2:

w/ad lib. Guitar Solo (use Guitar Solo 1 as a model for improv.)

Em | A | D | G | Em | D G

D | Em | A | D | G | Em | D G

Interlude:

D | Em | G

Acous. Gtr.

8va throughout
Mandolin (arr. for gtr.)

mf

1.2.3.4. *D*

5. *D*

Outro:

D | Em | G | D

Acous. Gtr. & Mandolin cont. simile

Mag-gie, I wish I'd nev-er seen your face.

Em | G | D

I'll

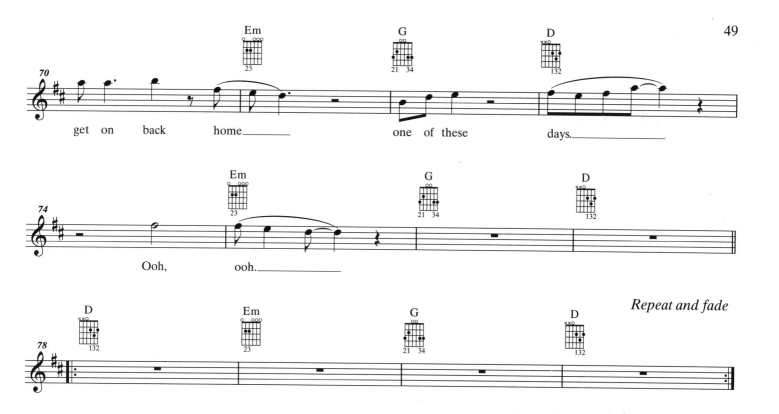

Verse 2:
The morning sun, when it's in your face,
Really shows your age.
But that don't worry me none,
In my eyes you're everything.
I laughed at all of your jokes,
My love you didn't need to coax.
Oh, Maggie, I couldn't have tried anymore.
You lead me away from home
Just to save you from being alone.
You stole my soul and that's a
Pain I can do without.

Verse 3:
All I needed was a friend
To lend a guiding hand.
But you turned into a lover and, mother,
What a lover, you wore me out.
All you did was wreck my bed,
And in the morning kick me in the head.
Oh, Maggie, I couldn't have tried anymore.
You lead me away from home
'Cause you didn't want to be alone.
You stole my heart,
I couldn't leave you if I tried.
(To Guitar Solo 1:)

Verse 4:
I suppose I could collect my books
And get on back to school.
Or steal my daddy's cue,
And make a living out of playing pool.
Or find myself a rock and roll band
That needs a helping hand.
Oh, Maggie, I wish I'd never seen your face.
You made a first-class fool out of me,
But I'm as blind as a fool can be.
You stole my heart
But I love you anyway.
(To Guitar Solo 2:)

Verse 2:
You've been learnin', and baby, I mean learnin'.
All them good times, baby, baby, I've been yearnin'.
Way, way down inside, honey, you need it.
I'm gonna give you my love.
I'm gonna give you my love.
(To Chorus:)

Verse 3:
You've been coolin', baby, I've been droolin'.
All the good times, baby, I've been misusin'.
Way, way down inside, I'm gonna give you my love.
I'm gonna give you every inch of my love.
Gonna give you my love.
(To Chorus:)

TABLATURE EXPLANATION
TAB illustrates the six strings of the guitar.
Notes and chords are indicated by the placement of fret numbers on each string.

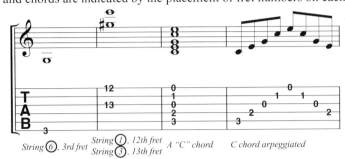

String ⑥, 3rd fret   String ①, 12th fret   A "C" chord   C chord arpeggiated
                     String ③, 13th fret

BENDING NOTES

Half Step: Play the note and bend string one half step (one fret).

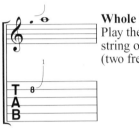

Whole Step: Play the note and bend string one whole step (two frets).

Slight Bend/ Quarter-Tone Bend: Play the note and bend string sharp.

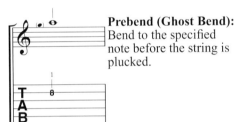

Prebend (Ghost Bend): Bend to the specified note before the string is plucked.

Prebend and Release: Play the already-bent string, then immediately drop it down to the fretted note.

Unison Bend: Play both notes and immediately bend the lower note to the same pitch as the higher note.

Bend and Release: Play the note and bend to the next pitch, then release to the original note. Only the first note is attacked.

Bends Involving More Than One String: Play the note and bend the string while playing an additional note on another string. Upon release, relieve the pressure from the additional note allowing the original note to sound alone.

Bends Involving Stationary Notes: Play both notes and immediately bend the lower note up to pitch. Release bend as indicated.

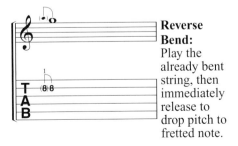

Reverse Bend: Play the already bent string, then immediately release to drop pitch to fretted note.

Unison Bend: Play both notes and immediately bend the lower note to the same pitch as the higher note.

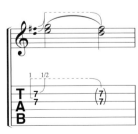

Double Note Bend: Play both notes and immediately bend both strings simultaneously up the indicated intervals.

ARTICULATIONS

 **Hammer On (Ascending Slur):** Play the lower note, then "hammer" your finger to the higher note. Only the first note is plucked.

 **Pull Off (Descending Slur):** Play the higher note with your first finger already in position on the lower note. Pull your finger off the first note with a strong downward motion that plucks the string—sounding the lower note.

 **Legato Slide:** Play the first note and, keeping pressure applied on the string, slide up to the second note. The diagonal line shows that it is a slide and not a hammer-on or a pull-off.

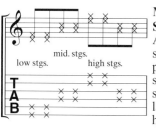 **Muted Strings:** A percussive sound is produced by striking the strings while laying the fret hand across them.

 **Palm Mute:** The notes are muted (muffled) by placing the palm of the pick hand lightly on the strings, just in front of the bridge.

 **Left Hand Hammer:** Using only the left hand, hammer on the first note played on each string.

 **Glissando:** Play note and slide in specified direction.

 **Bend and Tap Technique:** Play note and bend to specified interval. While holding bend, tap onto fret indicated with a "t."

 **Fretboard Tapping:** Tap onto the note indicated by the "t" with a finger of the pick hand, then pull off to the following note held by the fret hand.

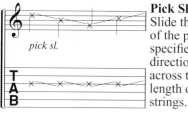 **Pick Slide:** Slide the edge of the pick in specified direction across the length of the strings.

 **Tremolo Picking:** The note or notes are picked as fast as possible.

 **Trill:** Hammer on and pull off consecutively and as fast as possible between the original note and the grace note.

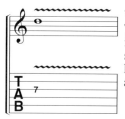 **Vibrato:** The pitch of a note is varied by a rapid shaking of the fret-hand finger, wrist, and forearm.

 **Accent:** Notes or chords are to be played with added emphasis.

Staccato (Detached Notes): Notes or chords are to be played about half their noted value and with separation.

HARMONICS

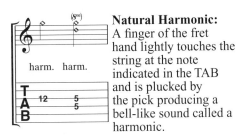

Natural Harmonic: A finger of the fret hand lightly touches the string at the note indicated in the TAB and is plucked by the pick producing a bell-like sound called a harmonic.

Artificial Harmonic: Fret the note at the first TAB number, lightly touch the string at the fret indicated in parens (usually 12 frets higher than the fretted note), then pluck the string with an available finger or your pick.

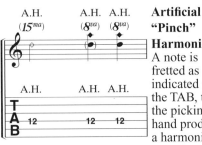

Artificial "Pinch" Harmonic: A note is fretted as indicated in the TAB, then the picking hand produces a harmonic by squeezing the pick firmly while using the tip of the index finger in the pick attack. If parenthesis are found around the fretted note, it does not sound. No parenthesis means both the fretted note and the A.H. are heard simultaneously.

RHYTHM SLASHES

Strum Marks/ Rhythm Slashes: Strum with the indicated rhythm pattern. Strum marks can be located above the staff or within the staff.

Single Notes with Rhythm Slashes: Sometimes single notes are incorporated into a strum pattern. The circled number below is the string and the fret number is above.

TREMOLO BAR

Specified Interval: The pitch of a note or chord is lowered to the specified interval and then return as indicated. The action of the tremolo bar is graphically represented by the peaks and valleys of the diagram.

Unspecified Interval: The pitch of a note or chord is lowered, usually very dramatically, until the pitch of the string becomes indeterminate.

PICK DIRECTION

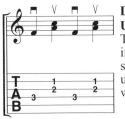

Downstrokes and Upstrokes: The downstroke is indicated with this symbol (⊓) and the upstroke is indicated with this (V).